NEW VANGUARD • 116

SIKORSKY UH-60 BLACK HAWK

CHRIS BISHOP   ILLUSTRATED BY IAN PALMER

First published in Great Britain in 2008 by Osprey Publishing,
Midland House, West Way, Botley, Oxford, OX2 0PH, UK
443 Park Avenue South, New York, NY 10016, USA
E-mail: info@ospreypublishing.com

A CIP catalog record for this book is available from the British Library

ISBN: 978 1 84176 852 6

Page layout by: Melissa Orrom Swan, Oxford
Index by Alan Thatcher
Typeset in Sabon and Myriad Pro
Originated by PDQ Digital Media Solutions
Printed in China through Worldprint Ltd.

08 09 10 11 12   10 9 8 7 6 5 4 3 2 1

FOR A CATALOG OF ALL BOOKS PUBLISHED BY OSPREY MILITARY AND
AVIATION PLEASE CONTACT:

NORTH AMERICA
Osprey Direct, c/o Random House Distribution Center, 400 Hahn Road,
Westminster, MD 21157
E-mail: info@ospreydirect.com

ALL OTHER REGIONS
Osprey Direct UK, P.O. Box 140 Wellingborough, Northants, NN8 2FA, UK
E-mail: info@ospreydirect.co.uk

Osprey Publishing is supporting the Woodland Trust, the UK's leading
woodland conservation charity, by funding the dedication of trees.

www.ospreypublishing.com

GLOSSARY

A2C2S	Army Airborne Command & Control System
AFCS	Automated Flight Computer System
CSAR	Combat Search and Rescue
ESSS	External Stores Support System
ETS	External Tank System
FLIR	forward-looking infrared
GPS/INS	Global Positioning System/Inertial Navigation System
HIRSS	Hover Infrared Suppression System
IR	Infrared
MEDEVAC	medical evacuation
NVG	night vision goggle
SEAL	Navy sea, air, and land team
UTTAS	Utility Tactical Transport Aircraft System

EDITOR'S NOTE

For ease of comparison between types, imperial measurements are used
almost exclusively throughout this book. The following data will help in
converting the imperial measurements to metric:

1 mile = 1.6km

1lb = 0.45kg

1 yard = 0.9m

1ft = 0.3m

1in. = 2.54cm/25.4mm

1 gal = 4.5 liters

1 ton (US) = 0.9 tonnes

CONTENTS

SIKORSKY UH-60 BLACK HAWK

INTRODUCTION

The Sikorsky corporation calls the UH-60 Black Hawk "America's helicopter." It has been in service for more than a quarter of a century, and with more than 1,500 Black Hawks on active duty with Regular Army and National Guard units around the world, it is the backbone of the United States Army's military helicopter fleet. Tough, reliable, and with excellent performance, the Black Hawk has been used for a wide variety of missions, from combat to peacekeeping, through drug interdiction to disaster relief. It is even used to fly the President.

Black Hawks are expected to operate anywhere in the world. Able to carry up to 11 troops, they can fly and fight in conditions ranging from hot and high desert conditions to the freezing cold and hurricane-force winds of the Arctic.

The versatility of the Black Hawk means that it can fly virtually any kind of mission the Army requires of it, from troop transport and combat assault through to resupply and combat support to artillery transport and electronic warfare. Black Hawks serve as flying ambulances, Special Forces transports, and command-and-control platforms. They transport everything from food and ammunition to fuel and personnel. As a utility helicopter, it is one of the best in the world.

The Black Hawk is a highly effective helicopter, even though its basic design dates back more than three decades. It has been the subject of numerous upgrades aimed to keep the aircraft at the forefront of battlefield capability. One of the most important developments has been the introduction of new, more powerful engines, which, when allied to a more rugged gearbox and toughened flight controls originally developed for the naval variant of the design, the SH-60 Seahawk, allow the L model of the Black Hawk to take off at a maximum gross weight of 22,000lb.

The ability to withstand battle damage was one of the key requirements for the original Army specification for the Black Hawk, with the capability to keep flying in the face of high-explosive cannon shells of up to 23mm being an essential feature of its construction. The Black Hawk airframe is versatile, and the type has been adapted to a variety of missions including special operations, maritime search and rescue, and VIP transport.

OPPOSITE
A Customs and Border Patrol Black Hawk swoops down on suspected lawbreakers near the southwest border of the United States. Originally delivered to track down drug smugglers, these Black Hawks in their black and gold trim are also used to monitor illegal immigrants. (US Customs and Border Patrol)

The Black Hawk originated in the 1970s to meet the requirements of the US Army's UTTAS (Utility Tactical Transport Aircraft System). In 1972 and 1973, Sikorsky used this mock-up to refine its design, making sure that it offered significant improvements over the Bell UH-1 Huey it was designed to replace. (Cody Images)

DEVELOPMENT

The transport helicopter has revolutionized the field of battle in the speed and precision with which it can deliver troops into combat. In June 1944, as Allied troops were forcing their way onto the beaches of occupied France in Normandy, they were preceded and aided by thousands of paratroopers, with many more air assault troops and their equipment delivered by assault glider. Airborne and air assault troops made a key contribution to victory, but at a fearful cost.

The future of airborne forces seemed in doubt after the end of World War II. Nearly every major parachute operation during the war had led to heavy casualties. But paratroopers were still the only military formations able to attack at speed over long distances. In the absence of anything better, paratroopers remained a key part of any army's force structure. However, air assault operations were about to take a quantum leap forward.

The potential for transport helicopters, possibly armed, to deliver troops into battle while under fire was quickly recognized. Developed in the 1940s, practical helicopters offered the potential to deliver troops, equipment, and supplies into the combat zone, bypassing enemy defenses by flying over them.

Limited operations during the Korean War were followed with some success by the British in Malaya, and by the French in Algeria. However, early helicopters were underpowered, carried relatively small payloads, and were unreliable.

 UH-60A/L

Standard UH-60 Black Hawks in US service have had very few color schemes applied in service, most being completed in Overall Helo Drab (Federal Standard paint 34031). This example is operated by the California Army National Guard, which has two companies of the 1st Battalion, 140th Aviation Regiment equipped with troop-carrying UH-60A/Ls based at Los Alamitos. The 126th Medical Company (Air Ambulance) operates the same type of helicopter, as well as a number of HH-60Ls out of Mather Field. The California Guard units have deployed in support of regular army units to the Balkans, Iraq, and Afghanistan, as well as providing support for state authorities on lifesaving, search-and-rescue, and firefighting missions.

Having watched the British and French use helicopters effectively in Suez, Malaya, and Algeria, the US Army set about developing its own heliborne assault concept. Recalling that a British Army officer in Borneo once said, "Six helicopters and sixty soldiers are worth more to me in the jungle than six hundred soldiers on foot," the US Army set about forming a completely helicopter-equipped formation, the 1st Air Cavalry Division.

Fortunately, the development of turbine-powered helicopters with increased reliability and better lifting capacity came just in time to make the idea of heliborne armies a truly practical proposition.

The image of the Bell UH-1 Huey flying into a hot landing zone in Southeast Asia is one of the enduring icons of the Vietnam War. Thousands of Hueys served in the war zone, taking every kind of soldier into and out of battle. The Huey series of helicopters served the US Army very well in Vietnam, but even as the conflict was heating up in the mid-1960s, the Army was beginning to think about a replacement.

The pioneering Bell UH-1 Huey had shown that turbine-powered helicopters were a vast improvement on first generation rotary-winged machines, but the Huey was far from an ideal battlefield machine. Although it served with distinction in Vietnam, it proved to be vulnerable to ground fire, and, in the late 1960s, the Army began to evolve a requirement for a new, more battle-worthy machine that would eventually replace the UH-1.

The requirement emerged in January 1972 as the Utility Tactical Transport Aircraft System (UTTAS) program. Manufacturers were asked to submit proposals for a new machine that would carry heavier loads at greater speeds and over greater distances than the Huey. At the same time, the design was to provide better protection and durability than the earlier helicopter.

Several companies offered proposals. The two finalists in the competition were Boeing Vertol and Sikorsky. Both were asked to build five prototypes, three of which were to be flying examples and two that were to be used for ground testing. Sikorsky had already started a series of experiments to look for possible technologies that would be of use in the new helicopter, using modified S-61 and S-65 transport helicopters, and the company had also begun development of a gunship helicopter, the S-67.

Using the lessons learned from these experimental programs, Sikorsky developed a design that was given the company designation S-70. Boeing Vertol's competing design, which was to have a composite main rotor, was the Model 237. The two designs were given the military designations YUH-60A and YUH-61A respectively. Both were to be powered by twin General Electric T700 engines. The UH-60A prototype first flew on October 17, 1974, with the YUH-61A following six weeks later on November 29.

The new helicopter was going to be extremely important to the US Army, so the evaluation program that began in 1976 was exceptionally thorough. The Sikorsky machine demonstrated the toughness and survivability that was a particularly important Army requirement when one of the prototypes crash-landed while on trials. On earlier designs, the chances were that the crew would have been seriously injured, but they survived this crash unharmed. The Army was also impressed by the fact that the machine flew from the crash site under its own power once its rotor blades had been replaced.

On December 23, 1976, the Army announced that Sikorsky had won the UTTAS competition. An initial contract was issued for three preproduction aircraft and 15 production UH-60As, and the new type was given the name Black Hawk. The first production helicopter flew in October 1978, and it entered operational service with the 101st Air Assault Division in summer 1979. The type's combat debut came in Grenada in 1983, where it proved as resistant to battle damage as the Army had hoped. In one incident, a flight of Black Hawks came under fierce machine-gun and cannon fire from the ground, surviving an antiaircraft fire onslaught which would probably have destroyed a flight comprising Bell UH-1 Hueys.

Faster, tougher, and much more capable than the UH-1 it replaced, the Black Hawk is now the US Army's most important utility transport helicopter. It provides the bulk of vertical troop-lift capability for Army divisions of all types.

The UH-60A is of conventional design with a large four-bladed main rotor, and a small four-bladed tail rotor. A combined tailplane and elevator, known as a stabilator, was mounted high on the tail fin in early prototypes, but was moved to the base of the fin in production aircraft. The main rotor blades are very tough, which enables them to survive hits from explosive cannon rounds. The strength comes from the use of composite and glass-reinforced plastic materials wrapped round a titanium spar, and to protect against damage from branches, the leading edge is sheathed with nickel. The composite tail rotor is tilted 20 degrees from the vertical, partly to reduce the noise it generates.

The Black Hawk began to enter service with the US Army in significant numbers early in the 1980s, deploying overseas to Germany and on exercises throughout the world. Here, a UH-60A MEDEVAC helicopter flies over the Great Pyramids near Cairo, Egypt, during Exercise *Bright Star*, 1983. (DoD)

The US Army evaluation of the UH-60 design concluded that it met nearly all of the requirements of the UTTAS design. It was faster and more robust than the Bell UH-1 Huey, and could carry more troops and heavier loads over longer distances than its predecessor. (Sikorsky)

The initial prototype differed from production machines in having a fixed swept stabilator, which tended to cause the helicopter to nose up and led to a series of experiments for alternate configurations. It was also fitted with a retractable tail wheel, and had a different fuselage and engine exhaust configuration.

Modern weaponry needs to be transported by air to allow for rapid deployment around the world. A feature of the original UTTAS requirement was that the new helicopter should be able to fit into standard USAF transport aircraft with a minimum of disassembly. The long, low design of the UH-60 and the low-set main rotor allow the helicopter to fit into the cargo bay of a Lockheed C-130 Hercules simply by folding its rotor blades. The C-130 can carry one Black Hawk, the Lockheed C-141B Starlifter can carry two, and the Lockheed C-5 Galaxy can carry six. The Starlifter has been replaced by the Boeing C-17 Globemaster II, a much larger aircraft with the capacity to carry three or four UH-60s.

The UH-60A is powered by twin General Electric T700-GE-700 turboshaft engines. These are designed to provide 1,560shp each. Like the rest of the Black Hawk, the engines are incredibly tough. They are designed to operate for at least 30 minutes, even after suffering battle damage sufficient to drain all of the engine oil. To start the main engines and for providing power on the ground, a T62T-40-1 auxiliary power unit (APU) able to deliver 100shp is mounted between the main engines. As a further exercise in strengthening, the fuel tanks are armored against small-arms fire and are also crash-resistant. Maximum speed is 163mph, though the normal operating maximum is 145mph. Maximum range with standard fuel and with no reserves is about 365 miles.

The UH-60A has wheeled landing gear, featuring heavy-duty shock absorbers designed to take up the impact of a hard landing without causing damage. The three wheels are in tail dragger configuration, with two at the front and one at the rear of fuselage. The helicopter can also be fitted with wide ski-style pads, enabling the machine to operate from swampy ground or from snow and ice.

The UH-60A carries a crew of three, including two pilots and a crew chief/gunner, all of whom are provided with armored seats resistant to 23mm cannon fire. Normal passenger capacity is for 11 fully equipped infantrymen, though in an emergency the Black Hawk can carry up to 20 passengers. By removing eight troop seats, the helicopter can be configured to carry four litters in the medical evacuation (MEDEVAC) role. The cabin is fitted with sliding doors on both sides.

External loads can also be carried: the UH-60A has a belly sling hook with a capacity of up to 8,000lb. This is enough to enable the Black Hawk to lift a 105mm artillery piece or a Hummer vehicle.

For self-defense, a machine gun can be pintle-mounted in a slide-open window on each side of the helicopter just behind the cockpit. This helps reduce clutter in the doorways, reflecting combat experience with the Bell UH-1 when door guns obstructed troops trying to deploy under fire. Initially, M-60D 7.62mm machine guns on the M144 armament subsystem were mounted, but these were later replaced by General Electric M134 7.62mm six-barreled Gatling-type miniguns or by the M240 variant of the FN MAG machine gun. The helicopter can also carry the M130 general purpose dispenser, which deploys chaff and infrared jamming flares.

VARIANTS

The original UH-60A model first became operational with the US Army in 1978, and the type continued to be delivered until 1989. It was then replaced in production by the UH-60L, an upgraded variant of the Black Hawk fitted with more powerful engines that delivered a quarter more power than the UH-60A. Over the next eight years, the Army took delivery of over 480 UH-60Ls, and, by the end of 1997, had received over 1,460 Black Hawks of both types. Delivery of at least 60 of the upgraded helicopters continued each year into the 21st century.

Elements of the US Army Aviation UH-60A/L Black Hawk helicopter fleet began reaching the end of their planned service life of 25 years in 2002. A Service Life Extension Program (SLEP) was planned for the UH-60 beginning in FY99 (Fiscal Year 1999). The program was intended to ensure the Black Hawk could meet its battlefield requirements into the third decade of the 21st century.

First flown in September 2003, the improved UH-60M offered significant performance enhancements over the preceding UH-60L. Initially approved in 2001, the Army announced that the bulk of the Black Hawk fleet – some 1,500 helicopters – would be brought up to the new standard. However, with many Black Hawk airframes beginning to show their age, it was decided that a mass upgrade would not be cost effective, and old airframes would instead be replaced by new-build aircraft.

Early Black Hawks could carry up to 8,000lb as a slung load. Here, a US Army UH-60 Black Hawk and a CH-47 Chinook are used to test new, longer slings and transport systems at Fort Campbell, Kentucky, in 2001. (DoD/Marshall W. Woods)

A large proportion of the US Army's UH-60 fleet is now flown by National Guard units. Here, the crew of a North Carolina Army National Guard Black Hawk begins a search-and-rescue exercise in cooperation with local fire departments and emergency medical services. (DoD/TSgt Brian E. Christiansen)

Even without the projected SLEP, the UH-60 fleet has undergone a wide range of improvements over the years.

To help protect the helicopter from heat-seeking guided missiles, engine exhaust shielding was fitted. The Infrared (IR) Cruise Suppression System, identifiable from its square exhaust, worked while the helicopter was in forward flight, but the helicopter was still vulnerable when hovering. From 1980, General Electric began to develop a more effective system, and, in 1989, the Hover Infrared Suppression System (HIRSS) was introduced.

Defensive countermeasures became increasingly important as the threat from enemy missiles grew. Some, but not all, UH-60s have been fitted with the AN/ALQ-144 "disco light" jammer to confound heat-seeking missiles. In high-threat environments, the helicopters have also carried AN/APR-39(V)1 and AN/APR-44 radar warning receivers (RWRs) and AN/ALE-39 chaff/flare dispensers, mounted on the forward end of the tail boom.

B

1. PROTOTYPE YUH-60

The YUH-60 flew for the first time on October 17, 1974. Although generally meeting the US Army's UTTAS requirements, the prototype aircraft was not without its problems, reliability being less than optimal and vibration being greater than expected. Part of the problem was traced to the low-mounted main rotor, designed for ease of loading aboard transport aircraft such as the Lockheed C-130 Hercules, and thus production aircraft were completed with the rotor mounted higher. A second problem was the fixed swept tailplane, which introduced a tendency for the prototypes to nose up in flight. Several different types of tailplane were tested, the most effective being the straight, moveable stabilator seen on all production aircraft.

2. EH-60 QUICK FIX

Electronic warfare has become a key part of any modern battlefield. The EH-60 Quick Fix variant of the Black Hawk was developed to provide commanders at divisional, brigade, and aviation regiment levels with their own electronic warfare capability. The original Quick Fix system was based on the standard UH-60A. Introduced in the 1980s, the helicopters were fitted with the AN/ALQ-151 special purpose countermeasure system that can be used either passively, to intercept enemy transmissions and to locate transmitters, or actively, to jam enemy communications. In the 1990s, it was announced that the EH-60s would be brought up to EH-60L standard, but the program was canceled in 1999 after only a handful of helicopters had been upgraded. The Quick Fix EH-60s carry the same color scheme as standard Black Hawks but are easily identifiable by the numerous antennae required by their electronic systems.

B

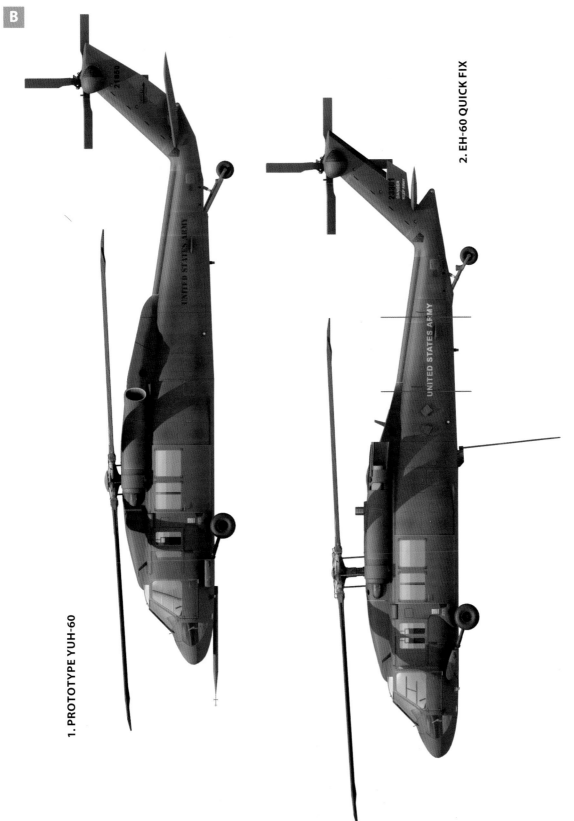

1. PROTOTYPE YUH-60

2. EH-60 QUICK FIX

An External Stores Support System (ESSS) field upgrade kit was developed. Originally designed for the carriage of external fuel tanks to allow the UH-60A to deploy across intercontinental ranges, the ESSS comprises graphite-epoxy composite stub wings with a total of four pylons. The pylons are primarily designed for the carriage of external fuel tanks, with a 450-gallon tank on each inboard pylon, and a 230-gallon tank on each outboard pylon. With a full load of external tanks, the UH-60A has a range of 1,325 miles.

The stub wings were also tested as weapons carriers, and they could be used to carry up to 10,000lb of ordnance, including rocket pods, antiarmor missiles, cannon pods, or mine dispensers.

The ESSS entered service in early 1986, but almost immediately it was found that a full load of tanks blocked the field of fire of the helicopter's door guns. Upswept stub wings known as the External Tank System (ETS) cured the problem, though only two external tanks could be fitted.

Other equipment that can be fitted to UH-60s includes removable Kevlar armor sheets, introduced after the Grenada operation when a number of casualties were caused by small-arms fire penetrating the floor; a kit that could convert standard UH-60s into MEDEVAC aircraft featuring four litters, three seats for walking wounded, additional lighting and extra storage for medical items; a swing-out rescue hoist; and improved avionics, including a Global Positioning System/Inertial Navigation System (GPS/INS) set. Some Black Hawks have been seen with cable cutter blades developed by Bristol Aerospace of Canada.

Fourteen UH-60As were transferred to the US Customs Service for drug enforcement duties. These machines are standard UH-60As, though they are fitted with a "Nitesun" searchlight and a forward-looking infrared (FLIR) turret. They are known informally to their crews as "Pot Hawks" and are painted black with dark gold trim. Other customs Service UH-60As are used on the southern border of the United States to deter illegal immigrants.

A number of examples of the original UH-60A have been delivered for experimental and training purposes, two having been used by the US Navy Test Pilots' School at Patuxent River, Maryland. Several aircraft serve as flying test beds under the designation JUH-60A. They are used to research new equipment and avionics. One helicopter, known as the Light Hawk, has been fitted with a fiber-optic control system that uses lasers to carry commands to the engines and flying surfaces. Nonflying examples used to instruct aircrew and engineers on the ground are known as GUH-60As.

UH-60L

A total of 974 UH-60As had been delivered to the US Army up to 1989. However, the many extra features that had been added to the first production variant of the Black Hawk had increased the overall weight of the machine, and the extra weight was degrading performance.

In the mid-1980s, Sikorsky began the development of a more powerful version of the Black Hawk, which was designated the UH-60L. Externally very similar to the UH-60A, the L variant was fitted with a pair of the more powerful General Electric T700-GE-701C turboshaft engines. These could each deliver a maximum of 1,900shp, though full power was only used in single-engine operations. The helicopter's transmission system was uprated and was capable of delivering a total of 3,400shp to the main rotor. Offering increased reliability and greatly enhanced performance in adverse conditions, the T700-GE-701C powers both the UH-60M and the AH-64D Apache.

All of the improvements that were applied to the UH-60A during its service were fitted to the UH-60L as standard during manufacture. The first UH-60Ls retained the UH-60A flight control system, but this could not cope with the extra power of the new engines, so a tougher and more sophisticated system was fitted to the new model. The Automatic Flight Control System (AFCS) had been developed for the naval version of the Sikorsky design, the S-70B or SH-60 Seahawk, which operated in a more challenging environment than the land-based variants. The new flight control system and an increase in the tail rotor pitch were more than enough to allow the UH-60L to take advantage of the more powerful engines and more efficient power train. Fatigue life of parts has been extended to at least 5,000 hours before replacement.

The first flight of the production UH-60L took place on March 22, 1988, with service deliveries beginning in October 1989. By the beginning of 2002, the US Army had 539 UH-60Ls in service.

A UH-60L of the California National Guard hovers over floodwaters. Rescue and disaster relief are important tasks assigned to the Army helicopter force, and the National Guard has a state mission to provide disaster relief. (Sikorsky)

A MEDEVAC UH-60L lifts off from a base in Bosnia. All Black Hawks can be converted to carry casualties, but the specialized ambulance variants like the UH-60Q and the HH-60L carry a much more extensive suite of medical equipment and casualty-handling gear in their cabins. (Sikorsky)

Externally, the UH-60L and the UH-60A are virtually identical. However, the upgrade has dramatically increased the helicopter's capability: the UH-60L's external payload was increased from 8,000lb to 9,000lb, and the new variant could carry the maximum load over 70 miles in hot and high conditions where the original model's capability was reduced by about 25 percent in such circumstances.

The increase in lifting ability was essential to enable the Black Hawk to handle the increasing weights of ground equipment like the M1036 weapons carrier model of the High Mobility Multipurpose Wheeled Vehicle (HMMWV). The helicopter is cleared to take off at a maximum gross weight of 22,000lb, though normal mission takeoff weight is around 17,500lb.

The UH-60L can be fitted with the ESSS developed for the UH-60A. The removable stub wings and pylons are primarily used for their designed purpose, to carry additional fuel tanks for extended range deployments of up to 1,150 nautical miles. The ESSS retains the theoretical ability to carry a heavy weapons load on four hardpoints, including up to 16 Hellfire antitank missiles. Sikorsky has also shown that the Black Hawk can store a further 16 Hellfires internally, making the UH-60L potentially one of the most heavily armed antiarmor platforms in service anywhere in the world.

UH-60M

In April 2001, the US Army approved an upgrade program to rebuild more than 1,500 UH-60A and UH-60L Black Hawks to a new standard to be designated the UH-60M. The first flight of the UH60M took place in September 2003, and three helicopters were delivered for the test program.

One was an upgraded UH-60A, one was an upgraded UH-60L, and one was the new-build airframe. As a result of the evaluation program, the US Army has since opted for new-build helicopters rather than upgrading existing airframes.

The new helicopter entered low-rate initial production (LRIP) in April 2005. The LRIP contract was for 22 new UH-60Ms to be delivered from July 2006, with initial operational evaluation (OPEVAL) beginning in September 2006. The model is now the standard production version of the Black Hawk for the US Army.

The UH-60M features new wide chord composite spar main rotor blades (which will provide 500lb more lift than the current UH-60L blade), a digitized 1553 bus-based glass cockpit and avionics suite with four multifunction displays, a four-axis fully coupled autopilot, an advanced flight control computer, an Embedded GPS Inertial (EGI) navigation system, a strengthened fuselage, and a more advanced infrared suppression.

Manufactured by Rockwell Collins, the high-tech glass cockpit carried by the latest versions of the Black Hawk is a far cry from the multitude of dials and switches used in earlier variants. The Special Forces variant is designed to have as much commonality as possible with other helicopters in the fleet, including the MH-47 and the MH-6. (Rockwell Collins)

The new General Electric T700-GE-701D engine is more powerful than the 701C, delivering up to 2,000shp, which provides additional lift during sling load operations. The internal fuel tanks have a capacity of 360 gallons. Auxiliary fuel can be carried – 370 gallons in two internal fuel tanks and 460 gallons externally.

The UH-60M retains the standard crew of three: the pilot and the copilot on the flight deck and a crew chief/gunner in the cabin. The helicopter is equipped with a glass cockpit and digital avionics. In addition, export customers for the Black Hawk, sold under the Sikorsky company's S-70 designation, can opt to have a digital Automated Flight Computer System (AFCS) fitted to simplify pilot workload. An Electronic Flight Information System (EFIS) provides primary flight control and navigation displays for the pilots.

As with earlier Black Hawks, the UH-60M is qualified as a launch platform for the laser-guided Hellfire antiarmor missile. The ESSS can carry a 10,000lb payload of missiles, rockets, cannon, and electronic countermeasures pods. The helicopter can also accommodate additional missiles, supplies, or personnel inside the cabin.

The external slung load capacity is similar to that of the preceding UH-60L, but the increased power means that the M variant can carry the maximum load in more hostile conditions or for longer distances. Among the weapons that can be transported is the M777A1 155mm Ultralightweight Field Howitzer now in service with the US Marine Corps.

UH-60 Firehawks

The UH-60 Firehawk is a development of the Black Hawk designed to provide the helicopter with both a wartime and peacetime firefighting capability. The main modification to the aircraft is the addition of a detachable 1,000-gallon belly tank to carry fire retardant. One of the key firefighting features of the helicopter is the retractable snorkel, developed

One of the first operational UH-60M Black Hawk helicopters arrives to drop off Iraqi Prime Minister Nouri al-Maliki and other dignitaries at the 7th Iraqi Army Division headquarters on Camp Blue Diamond, Iraq, March 13, 2007. (US Marine Corps/Sgt David J. Murphy)

by Aero Union and Sikorsky. The snorkel can draw water from depths as shallow as 18in. and can fill the belly tank in 50 seconds.

Designed for firefighting, rescue, medical evacuation, and external lift of bulky cargo and equipment, the Oregon National Guard was the first military organization to add the Firehawk to its inventory. The Los Angeles County Fire Department was the first municipal organization to do so. Military variants of the Firehawk retain the combat capabilities of the standard UH-60.

Electronic Hawks

In 1980, the US Army modified a single UH-60A as the YEH-60B Stand-Off Target Acquisition System (SOTAS) for battlefield surveillance. This machine featured extended main landing gear that straddled a long, rectangular box antenna for the Motorola SOTAS radar system. In operation, the main gear retracted upward, and the antenna rotated to scan the battlefield area. However, the Army decided to collaborate with the US Air Force on the much more capable E-8 Joint Stars battlefield surveillance system, based on the Boeing 707 airliner, and the SOTAS program was canceled in September 1981.

In the late 1970s, the Army decided to develop a variant of the Black Hawk as a battlefield electronic warfare platform, designed to locate, monitor, and jam enemy communications. A number of UH-60As were converted to the EH-60C configuration, which involved fitting the Tracor Quick Fix IIB electronic warfare system.

The YEH-60A prototype first flew on September 24, 1981. Production conversions were originally designated EH-60A, but were later redesignated EH-60C. The Army originally planned to acquire 130 EH-60Cs, but budget constraints meant that conversion was halted in 1988 after 66 were completed.

The EH-60C was easy to identify from the two large dipole antennae along each side of the tail boom, and the long whip antenna that could be pivoted down from the belly in flight. The EH-60C carried two operators along with pilot and copilot, and it featured a datalink system to download intelligence data to ground stations or other platforms.

In the late 1990s, seven EH-60Cs were upgraded to EH-60L Advanced Quick Fix configuration, with the airframes brought up to UH-60L. However, the program stalled, and it appears that nothing more was done with the EH-60L.

A2C2S

In order to provide senior commanders with a capable and highly mobile intelligence asset, the Army has fielded a new electronic variant of the Black Hawk. Originally designated the EH-60C Command and Control, it is now known as the Army Airborne Command & Control System (A2C2S). Primarily a communications platform, the A2C2S receives information from a wide variety of sources, including reconnaissance aircraft and unmanned aerial vehicles, and transmits it to ground-based command posts at battalion level or higher for further action. A2C2S prototypes have been used to support the operations of the US 4th Infantry Division in Iraq.

VH-60

Although the vast majority of Black Hawks generally provide only the most basic transport for combat troops, a small number of examples of the type offer considerably more comfort to their passengers. Nine Black Hawks were delivered to the US Marine Corps Squadron HMX-1 from 1989 to fly the President and his staff. The VH-60N Black Hawk is fitted with luxury seating and carries extra soundproofing, but comfort is only part of the story. The President has to be able to contact the national command authorities at all times, so the aircraft is fitted with a comprehensive communications suite. It is also fitted with a full range of defensive measures including chaff and flare dispensers and a sophisticated electronic countermeasures system.

Originally known as the VH-60A, the type was redesignated VH-60N in 1989. The VH-60Ns are used to support the President and his staff and are known as Presidential Hawks. Any aircraft carrying the President has the call sign Marine One.

UH-60Q MEDEVAC

All Black Hawks can be converted to carry casualties by removing seats and fitting casualty litters. However, modernizing the MEDEVAC system was the Army Surgeon General's number one priority in the early 1990s. The Army requested a specialized MEDEVAC version of the Black Hawk, the UH-60Q, to replace UH-60A/L machines configured for the MEDEVAC role.

Like the UH-60A/L MEDEVAC machines, the UH-60Q has accommodation for litters and medical attendants, but has space for a far more extensive suite of emergency medical gear. The UH-60Q provides a six-patient litter system, onboard oxygen generation, and a medical suction system. The cutting-edge technology incorporates an improved environmental control system, as well as cardiac monitoring systems.

Detachment 1 of the 146th Medical Co. (Air Ambulance) was established as the Combat Enhanced Capability Aviation Team (CECAT [Medical]) with the first YUH-60Q demonstrator in 1992. A slightly lighter and cheaper design was approved in 1994 by the Department of the Army, and the final shape of the helicopter was completed by Sikorsky in 1997.

US President Clinton salutes as he exits Marine One, a VH-60N Black Hawk helicopter, at Peterson Air Force Base, Colorado, in 1999. Introduced into presidential service in the late 1980s, the VH-60 has an extensive communications and electronic defense suite, together with a luxury cabin. It is the only Black Hawk in Marine Corps service. (DoD/SSgt Alex Lloyd, USAF)

Although a highly capable MEDEVAC design, the UH-60Q was not ordered in great numbers due to funding pressures. The four operational aircraft that were delivered are currently flying with the Tennessee National Guard. However, the requirement for a high-capability air ambulance remained pressing, and, in 2000, the Army contracted with Sikorsky to upgrade a number of UH-60Ls to HH-60L standard, providing a MEDEVAC machine with similar capabilities to the UH-60Q, with the ability to carry and care for up to six seriously ill patients and their medical attendants. Nine aircraft have been delivered to the 507th Medical Co. (Air Ambulance) and to the California and West Virginia National Guards.

Today's MEDEVAC, or Dustoff, Black Hawks are highly capable machines, but they are nevertheless only interim air ambulances pending production of the HH-60M. This variant has better performance and a fully integrated avionics fit. The Army has a requirement for 336 HH-60Ms and plans for just under a quarter of its new utility helicopters to be dedicated medical evacuation aircraft.

Special operations Hawks

Special Forces units have proliferated in most armies over the last 40 years, and helicopters are ideal platforms for delivering and supporting Special Forces teams. In the 1980s, the Army decided to convert 30 UH-60As to a special operations version, known as the MH-60A. This featured a number of modifications, some of which were later to be applied to other Black Hawk variants. The primary mission of the MH-60 is to conduct overt or covert infiltration, exfiltration, and resupply of Special Operations Forces across a wide range of environmental conditions.

To give the helicopter additional range, an in-flight refueling probe was fitted, and an additional 117-gallon internal fuel tank was mounted in the rear of the cabin. This gave the MH-60 an infiltration radius without air refueling of just under 340 miles. HIRSS exhaust shields were fitted to give protection against heat-seeking missiles, and other defensive counter-measures, including a disco light heat-seeking missile jammer and two M130 chaff/flare dispensers, were added.

C — HH/MH-60G PAVE HAWK

The increased speed, range, and carrying capacity of the Black Hawk meant that it quickly found a number of uses in the special operations community. The MH-60G Pave Hawk was designed to deliver and extract Special Forces behind enemy lines, while the similar HH-60G was developed as a combat rescue helicopter for the Air Force. Both types are equipped with weather radar to allow operations in poor weather, while pilots are equipped with night vision goggles (NVGs) that enable missions to be carried out in low visibility. Pave Hawks are equipped with retractable in-flight refueling probes and internal auxiliary fuel tanks for increased range. Both types have seen extensive combat since the end of the 1980s, flying missions in Operation *Desert Storm*, Operation *Iraqi Freedom*, and Operation *Enduring Freedom* in Afghanistan, as depicted here.

To enable the aircraft to operate by night, a night vision goggle (NVG)-compatible cockpit was fitted, and a FLIR video camera was mounted in a turret in the nose. Defensive capabilities were increased by adding a pintle-mounted minigun on each side in place of the M60D machine guns normally carried at the time.

Since many of its features were tacked on in an improvised fashion, the MH-60A was nicknamed the Velcro Hawk. These machines were replaced in regular Army service by UH-60Ls brought up to a similar MH-60L Velcro Hawk configuration. The older MH-60As were handed down to Army National Guard units.

As with most variants of the UH-60A and UH-60L, the MH-60s could be fitted with either the ETS or ESSS stub wings, and they have carried a variety of stores and armaments, including a 30mm chain gun and unguided rocket pods. Developed for the US Army's 160th Special Operations Aviation Regiment at Fort Campbell, Kentucky, armed MH-60Ls entered service in 1990. Designated as the MH-60L Direct Action Penetrator or Defensive Armed Penetrator (DAP), the armed MH-60 has the primary mission of armed escort and fire support.

MH-60K

The first MH-60s were considered interim platforms, serving until the MH-60K Black Hawk, optimized for special operations machines, could enter service. Development began in 1986, and 23 MH-60Ks entered service with the 160th Special Operations Aviation Regiment from 1990. The first helicopters were declared operational in 1995.

The MH-60K has all of the features of the earlier special operations helicopters, but additional features include improved sensors, including an AN/AAQ-16B FLIR turret, a radar altimeter for low-altitude flight, and a Texas Instruments AN/APQ-174 terrain-following radar, mounted under

Special Forces combat divers from the 7th Special Forces Group (Airborne) at Fort Bragg, North Carolina, fast-rope from an MH-60 Black Hawk helicopter onto the deck of a US Navy nuclear-powered submarine in the US Southern Command area of operations. (DoD)

a radome in the nose. Navigation and communications equipment was upgraded, and a much more comprehensive defensive countermeasures suite was added that included missile, radar, and laser warning detectors. Other defensive countermeasures include an AN/ALQ-136 pulse jammer and an AN/ALQ-162 radio frequency jammer.

A pintle mount for a .50-cal. machine gun was provided in each door. The heavy machine guns have a much lower rate of fire than the miniguns in the window mounts, but they have greater range and striking power. The MH-60K has been qualified to carry Stinger air-to-air missiles and Hellfire antiarmor missiles, mounted on the upswept ETS pylons.

The first MH-60K made its initial flight on August 10, 1990, and the first production conversion took to the air on February 26, 1992.

Air Force Hawks

In the early 1980s, the Air Force wanted to find a replacement for the Sikorsky S-61R/ HH-3E "Jolly Green Giant" and the Bell HH-1 Hueys then in service in the USAF Combat Search and Rescue (CSAR) role. In 1981, the Air Force obtained 11 UH-60As, with one to be converted as a prototype for a CSAR variant designated the MH-60D. The MH-60D specification was similar to the later Army MH-60K, with in-flight refueling probe, FLIR, radar, countermeasures suite, and armament capability. The initial MH-60D conversion flew on February 4, 1984, the first of what the Air Force hoped would be 243 MH-60Ds.

By that time, however, it was clear that funding would not be available for the advanced new rescue helicopters. The Air Force decided to cut its requirement to 89 MH-60Ds, supported by 66 HH-60Es. These were basically MH-60Ds without the all-weather capability. Even that was too much for the budget, and the program was canceled.

The Air Force then tried to acquire the HH-60A, which was basically an MH-60D with simpler avionics. The MH-60D prototype was modified to HH-60A configuration, making its first flight in its new form on July 3, 1985. However, even that was too expensive, and the HH-60A prototype ended up in storage.

D UH-60A

Designed to be a significant improvement over the UH-1 Huey it replaced, everything about the UH-60A Black Hawk is tough. From the four-bladed rotors wrapped around titanium spars to the twin General Electric T700-GE-700 turboshaft engines, the helicopter's components are designed to stand up to hard operational use and battle damage. The fuel tanks are armored against small-arms fire and the heavy-duty landing gear is designed to withstand hard landings. Vital areas such as the engines, the rotor systems, and the pilot seats are fitted with protective armor able to withstand direct hits from explosive 23mm cannon shells. However, in the initial design of the fuselage, fatigue was not specified as a design criterion. As a result, with early aircraft now reaching a quarter century, fatigue failures are being observed by many users.

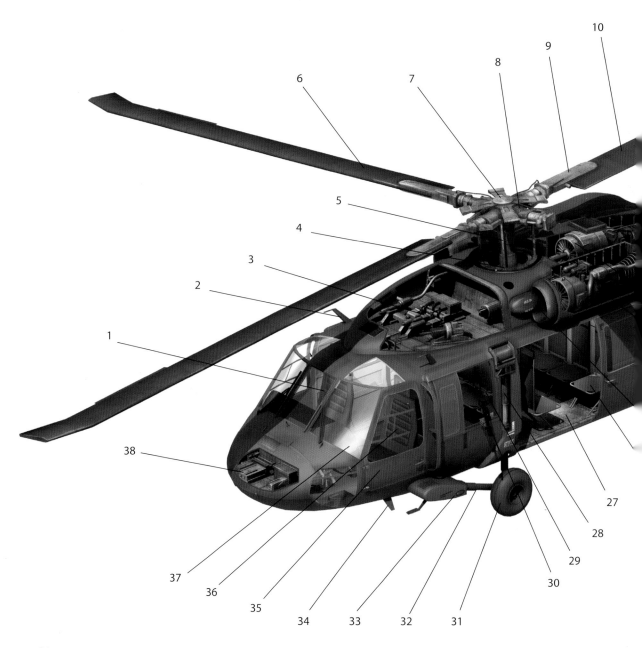

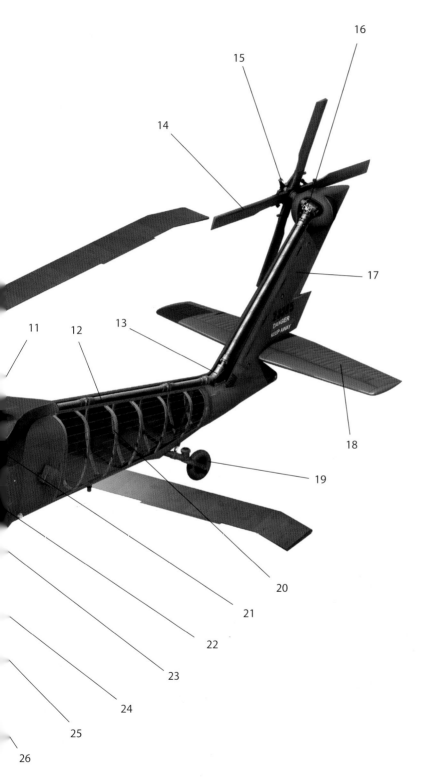

16

15

14

17

13

11   12

18

19

20

21

22

23

24

25

26

KEY

1   Pilot's armored seat
2   Pitot tube
3   Avionics bay
4   Blade pitch control swashplate
5   Blade pitch control rod
6   Nickel-plated rotor leading edge
7   Rotor head
8   Rotor attachment
9   Blade root attachment joint
10 Main rotor blade
11 UHF/VHF blade aerial
12 Tail rotor transmission shaft
13 Bevel drive gearbox
14 Inclined tail rotor
15 Tail rotor hub
16 Right angle gearbox
17 Tail fin
18 "Stabilator" combined stabilizer
    and elevator
19 Tail wheel
20 Tail boom frame construction
21 Exhaust nozzle
22 T62T-40-1 auxiliary power unit
23 General Electric T700-GE-700
    turboshaft engine
24 Main cargo door
25 Engine air intake
26 Passenger seats
27 Main cargo entrance
28 Main landing gear shock absorber
29 Window
30 Defensive gun mount
31 Port main wheel
32 Main landing gear leg
33 Navigation light
34 UHF blade aerial
35 Copilot's door
36 Copilot's armored seat
37 Windscreen
38 Nose equipment bay

In order to achieve some sort of combat rescue capability, the Air Force decided to develop a minimally modified UH-60A for the CSAR/special operations role. Designated the UH-60A Credible Hawk, the new design featured an extendable refueling probe, an internal 117-gallon fuel tank mounted in the rear of the cabin with space for a litter on top, provision for ESSS or ETS stub wings, and HIRSS exhaust shields. The GECAL M218 12.7mm three-barrel Gatling gun was qualified as a substitute for the 7.62mm M-60D or the GE minigun.

MH-60G Pave Hawk

The Pave Hawk is a twin-engine medium-lift helicopter operated by the Air Force Special Operations Command, a component of the US Special Operations Command. The basic crew normally consists of five: pilot, copilot, flight engineer, and two pararescuemen. The aircraft can also carry eight to ten troops. Pave Hawks are equipped with a rescue hoist with a 200ft cable and 600lb lift capacity.

The 98 Credible Hawks acquired in the 1980s were to be brought up to MH-60G Pave Hawk configuration in a two-phase program. Only 16 of the total of 98 MH-60Gs received the Phase 3 gear. These Pave Hawks were assigned the special operations role, while the other 82, with the Phase Two equipment fit, were assigned the CSAR role in October 1991 and redesignated HH-60G.

The Phase Two update included a Bendix-King 1400C navigation radar in a radome on the left side of the nose, an AN/ASN-137 Doppler radar, a GPS/INS set, a moving-map display, secure communications, and improved defensive countermeasures.

Eight US Army 173rd Airborne Brigade paratroopers sit in the open cargo bay doors of a UH-60 Black Hawk before making a low altitude static line training jump over Maniago, Pordenone Province, Italy. (DoD/SrA Priscilla Robinson, USAF)

The Phase Three update included an AN/AAQ-16 FLIR imager; a partial glass cockpit with twin flat-panel displays and a head-up display (HUD); a door mount on each side for a 12.7mm machine gun, along with the gun mount in each window; infrared lights for night refueling; and a ring laser gyro inertial navigation system.

The MH-60G's primary wartime missions are infiltration, exfiltration, and resupply of special operations forces in day, night, or marginal weather conditions. Other missions includeCSAR.

The HH-60G's primary mission is CSAR, though it can also be used in many of the roles performed by the more capable MH-60G. Low-level tactical flight profiles are used to avoid threats. NVG and FLIR assisted low-level night operations and night water operation missions are performed by specially trained crews.

A US Army Special Forces soldier jumps from a USA MH-60K Pave Hawk multimission helicopter during an infiltration training exercise off the coast of Naval Air Station, Key West, Florida. The MH-60K entered service with Special Operations Command in 1990 and became operational in 1995. (DoD/MC2 Timothy Cox, USN)

Future Hawks

The Army and Sikorsky are also in discussion over a follow up to the UH-60M, known as the Future Utility Rotorcraft (FUR), previously known as the UH-60X. While currently in the conceptual stages, the FUR is not necessarily based on the UH-60 airframe but lists as goals 175 knots cruise, 500nm radius, 10,000lb external lift capacity, improved handling qualities, and increased survivability.

The Sikorsky proposal for the FUR would use the rotor system, controls, and drive train from the Sikorsky S-92. The S-92 is based on proven Black Hawk technology, with an extended tail boom to allow the helicopter to deal with a wider rotor, more powerful engines, capacity to seat 22 troops, and a rear loading ramp. The H-92 Superhawk is the military variant of the S-92.

Currently, the requirements for the FUR are in the development stage at the Department of Combat Development, but a Black Hawk replacement is unlikely to be in service until 2025.

BLACK HAWKS IN ACTION

Grenada: Operation *Urgent Fury*

The UH-60's baptism of fire came in October 1983. The invasion of Grenada, Operation *Urgent Fury*, was an occupation of the island nation by the United States and several other nations in response to a *coup d'état* by Deputy Prime Minister Bernard Coard.

The invasion, starting at 0500hrs on October 25, was the first major operation conducted by the US military since the Vietnam War. The mission of the troops involved was to evacuate US citizens, neutralize any resistance, stabilize the situation, and maintain the peace.

At 0534hrs, the first US Army Rangers began dropping at Point Salines airfield, and less than two hours elapsed from the first drop until the last unit was on the ground, shortly after 0700hrs in the morning. At the end of the first day of action, the Rangers had secured the airfield and the True Blue campus at St George's Medical Center, at a cost of five dead and six wounded.

Once the Rangers had secured the runway, elements of the 82nd Airborne Division landed, and, late in the evening of the 26th, the Division's 3rd Brigade began to deploy across the island.

A US Air Force HH-60G Pave Hawk helicopter from the 66th Rescue Squadron, Nellis Air Force Base, Nevada, returns to Nellis after a mission over the Nevada Test and Training range. The HH-60 lacks the advanced glass cockpit fitted to the similar MH-60G. (DoD/TSgt Kevin J. Gruenwald, USAF)

The brigade was equipped with UH-60A Black Hawks. On October 27, the airborne troopers, with close air and naval gunfire support, moved against the Calivigny military barracks, east of Point Salines. The assault completed the last major objective for the peacekeeping forces.

The Black Hawk performed as well as could be expected, showing a much higher degree of resistance to battle damage than the earlier UH-1 Huey. One aircraft was hit 47 times but continued to fly, while another was hit five times in the fuel tanks. The self-sealing system ensured that the tanks did not leak.

However, casualties were taken when the floors of some of the Black Hawks were penetrated by enemy fire: it was as a result of this experience that the Army developed a Kevlar blanket which could be fitted to the deck of the helicopter's cabin for extra protection.

Panama: Operation *Just Cause*

Several months of tension between the United States and Panama, led by dictator General Manuel Noriega, came to a head at the end of 1989 with the killing of a US Marine officer when four US personnel were stopped at a roadblock outside the Panama Defense Force headquarters in the El Chorrillo neighborhood of Panama City.

President George H. W. Bush resolved to invade Panama, with the expressed aim to safeguard the lives of US citizens, to defend democracy and human rights in Panama, to protect the Panama Canal after Noriega threatened the neutrality of that vital waterway, and to counter the increasing

The Sikorsky S-92 Superhawk is an upgraded and enlarged helicopter evolution of the S-70 design. Three examples have been ordered as a presidential transport by Korea, but the type lost out in the competition to provide the next US presidential transport to the larger Lockheed Martin VH-71, a development of the Anglo-Italian EH101. (Sikorsky)

amount of drugs passing through the country. Panama had become a center for drug money laundering and a transit point for drug trafficking to the United States and Europe, and evidence pointed to Noriega's direct involvement in the business.

US Army forces, supported by the US Air Force and the US Navy, participated in Operation *Just Cause*. Ground forces equipped with UH-60s consisted of combat elements of the XVIII Airborne Corps, including the 82nd Airborne Division, the 7th Infantry Division (Light), the 75th Ranger Regiment, together with a Joint Special Operations Task Force, elements of the 5th Infantry Division, and the US Marines.

The operation involved 27,684 US troops and over 300 aircraft, including the F-117A Nighthawk stealth aircraft and the AH-64 Apache attack helicopter, which were seeing action for the first time. These were deployed against the 16,000 members of the Panama Defense Force (PDF). The operation began on December 20, 1989, at 0100hrs local time, with assaults on the civilian Punta Paitilla Airport in Panama City; a PDF garrison and airfield at Rio Hato, where Noriega also maintained a residence; and other military command centers throughout the country.

The attack on the central headquarters of the PDF (referred to as La Comandancia) touched off several fires, one of which destroyed most of the adjoining and heavily populated El Chorrillo neighborhood in downtown Panama City. During the firefight at La Comandancia, the PDF downed two special operations helicopters and forced one AH-6 "Little Bird" to crash land in the Panama Canal.

Operation *Just Cause* saw the first use of US Air Force MH-60G Pave Hawks in the special operations role. Deployed to Panama by the 55th Special Operations Squadron from Eglin AFB in Florida, a Pave Hawk and an MH-53J Pave Low were sent to deliver reinforcements to a Navy sea, air, and land team (SEAL) that had been dropped on Paitilla Airfield to prevent Noriega from fleeing the country by air. Flying in pitch blackness using NVGs, the Special Forces machines successfully delivered their reinforcements, and also picked up several wounded SEALs.

Iraq: Operation *Desert Storm*

The improved UH-60L was in service in time to fly alongside UH-60As in Operation *Desert Storm* during the Gulf War in 1991, with the Army deploying about 400 Black Hawks of various types to support the conflict. They were fitted with engine intake covers and other items to protect them from desert sand, and priority was given to implementing upgrades such as long-range fuel tanks and improved avionics.

Operation *Urgent Fury* in Grenada proved that the Black Hawk was considerably more resistant to battle damage than the Bell UH-1 that it replaced. These four helicopters were all hit by heavy enemy fire but survived, whereas the older Huey would most likely have been destroyed. (DoD/TSgt M. J. Creen)

Operation *Just Cause* in Panama saw the combat debut of the MH-60G Pave Hawk. Based at Eglin Air Force Base in Florida, the type was forward deployed to Howard Air Force Base in the Canal Zone, from where, along with MH-53J Pave Low helicopters, they supported the SEAL team attack on Paitilla Airfield. (DoD/TSgt Lee Schading)

On February 24, 1991, the first day of the ground war, Black Hawks were the primary element of the biggest single helicopter airlift in history to date, with a total of over 300 machines participating in a 101st Airborne Division assault on a site in the Iraqi desert codenamed Landing Zone Cobra.

The lead helicopters were from Company C of the 5th Battalion, 101st Aviation Regiment, which made their assault as dawn broke. This was at the request of the infantrymen, who felt that a night attack might have been confusing to the troops involved. Escorted by AH-64 Apache gunships, the helicopters made their attack at high speed, flying as low as 10 feet above the desert.

The Company C machines had been stripped of their troop seats to allow 15 rather than 11 fully equipped troopers to be carried. The lack of cabin obstruction meant that troops could exit the aircraft quickly. Once on the ground, the airborne troopers went to ground, to allow the helicopter door gunners a clear field of fire.

In the action that followed, some 350 Iraqi prisoners were taken, a bunker complex was destroyed, and Landing Zone Cobra was secured.

Special operations Black Hawks played a significant part in the combat. During *Desert Storm*, USAF Pave Hawks provided combat recovery for coalition air forces in Iraq, Saudi Arabia, Kuwait, and the Persian Gulf.

Black Hawks are considerably more powerful than the UH-1 Hueys they replaced. Here, a UH-60 of the 82nd Aviation Brigade prepares to lift off with a US Army M-102 105mm towed howitzer during Operation *Desert Shield*. (DoD/ Sgt Cumper)

They also provided emergency evacuation coverage for US Navy SEAL teams penetrating the Kuwaiti coast before the invasion.

The 1st Battalion of the 160th Special Operations Aviation Regiment (Airborne) was deployed to the desert in October 1990 to conduct special operations aviation missions against the Iraqi regime. During their 61-day deployment, they executed hundreds of missions deep into enemy airspace against targets that remain classified.

During one such operation on February 21, 1991, an MH-60L Black Hawk, flown by CW3 Michael Anderson and Capt Charles Cooper, responded to a request for an urgent medical evacuation deep in enemy territory under zero illumination.

They flew their aircraft at an extremely low altitude to evade the air defense artillery threat. In spite of dense fog – which they could not increase altitude to avoid, and against which their night vision equipment was useless – they continued the mission by relying on their experience using navigational instruments, and extracted a badly wounded soldier. Unfortunately while returning to the medical facility, they encountered a fierce sandstorm and lost visual reference with the ground, causing them to crash, killing both of the pilots and two crew chiefs.

In all, six Black Hawks were lost during the conflict, two due to combat action and the other four due to accidents.

During *Desert Storm*, coalition forces were supported by MEDEVAC Black Hawks operated by activated National Guard and Reserve units. The Army was charged with providing theater-wide care to the Navy, Air Force, Marine Corps, and special operations personnel.

Somalia: Operation *Continue Hope*

Black Hawks are a key part of any US Army combat deployment and have taken part in most US interventions since the Gulf War. One of the most noted engagements was the Somalia intervention in 1993. Operation *Continue Hope* provided support to United Nations attempts to protect humanitarian relief operations by supplying personnel, logistical, communications, intelligence support, a quick reaction force, and other elements as required.

Over 60 US Army aircraft and approximately 1,000 aviation personnel operated in Somalia from 1992 to 1994. On October 3, 1993, two Black

ABOVE LEFT
UH-60A Black Hawk helicopters prepare to take off as the 82nd Aviation Brigade of the 82nd Airborne Division relocates in the desert during Operation *Desert Shield*. Once the ground war started, the 82nd Airborne Division used the type to ferry troops forward in its deep penetration of Iraqi territory as coalition forces drove rapidly toward the River Euphrates. (DoD)

ABOVE RIGHT
The US Army deployed more than 400 UH-60 Black Hawks to Saudi Arabia in 1990 and 1991. Here, a Black Hawk prepares to follow two other helicopters into the air during the early stages of the US Army's deployment to Saudi Arabia in Operation *Desert Shield*. (DoD)

A US Army medical Black Hawk at Rinas, near Tirana in Albania, prepares for a training mission over Kosovo during Operation *Sustain Hope*. When they arrived in 1999, helicopter crews flew daily missions to familiarize themselves with the terrain. (DoD/TSgt Cesar Rodriguez)

Hawks were shot down by rocket-propelled grenades during a raid, and the crew of one was slaughtered and dragged through the streets, the incident becoming the basis for the well-known movie *Black Hawk Down*. The fighting that followed saw 18 US personnel dead and 78 wounded, along with over 1,000 Somali casualties.

Haiti: Operation *Uphold Democracy*

When Jean-Bertrand Aristide, the first democratically elected president of Haiti, was overthrown in a violent coup by General Raoul Cédras in 1991, it signaled the beginning of a period of oppressive military rule on the Caribbean island. Hundreds were killed in the coup, and as many as 5,000 Haitians were killed over the next two years. Tens of thousands fled the country. In 1994, with repression increasing, the United Nations authorized member states to use all necessary means to facilitate the departure of Haiti's military leadership and to restore Haiti's constitutionally elected government to power.

Operation *Uphold Democracy* got under way in September 1994 when a US-led multinational force prepared to invade Haiti. Elements of the 82nd Airborne Division were already in the air preparing to make a combat jump onto the island when the Haitian military government backed down and agreed to relinquish power.

Over 20,000 troops led by the US XVIII Airborne Corps occupied the island peacefully. Eighteen hundred troops of the 10th Mountain Division were transported along with their Black Hawks to Haiti aboard the nuclear-powered aircraft carrier USS *Dwight D. Eisenhower*. They occupied Port-au-Prince and provided logistical support to the Special Forces teams that had spread out through the country.

The peacekeeping mission was transferred to the United Nations on March 31, 1995, with 2,400 US troops remaining on the island to support UN operations with vehicle and helicopter logistics.

The Balkans

Black Hawks were used extensively to provide support to United Nations and NATO peacekeeping operations in the Balkans from 1995. The troubles had started early in 1992 when Bosnia-Herzegovina elected to secede from Yugoslavia. However, the minority Serb population disagreed and announced the creation of their own state. A bloody civil war broke out, and with the support of Serbia, the Bosnian Serbs occupied large areas of territory.

 HH-60G PAVE HAWK

The Special Forces and rescue variants of the Black Hawk have now been in service for two decades. A number of current aircraft are finished in Gunship Gray (Federal Standard paint 36118) for low-visibility daylight operations against a ground threat, gray being much less obvious against the sky than standard green or camouflage colors. This aircraft is fitted with the External Stores Support System (ESSS). Developed in the 1980s to allow aircraft to be ferried over long distances, the ESSS consists of two downward-sloping stub wings with four hardpoints for external tanks. The extra fuel carried allows rescue helicopters to penetrate deep into enemy territory, where aerial refueling might be risky. In combat (and as shown here), only the outer tanks are fitted, allowing a clear field of fire for the door gunners.

Soldiers of the US Army's 10th Mountain Division gather on the flight deck of the nuclear-powered aircraft carrier USS *Dwight D. Eisenhower* (CVN-69) as the ship gets underway from Norfolk, Virginia, for the Caribbean en route to Haiti for operations *Able Vigil* and *Support Democracy*. Several UH-60 Black Hawk helicopters are parked on the flight deck. (DoD/Ph2 Steve Enfield)

A lightly armed UN Protection Force (UNPROFOR) was deployed but had little effect. The UN was eventually forced to launch Operation *Deliberate Force* in August 1995, bombing targets around Sarajevo and in other areas held by the Bosnian Serbs. The attacks encouraged a combined offensive by the Bosnian Muslims and Bosnian Croats to push the Bosnian Serbs back from areas that they had conquered at the beginning of the civil war.

On November 21, the warring factions met in Dayton, Ohio, to sign an agreement to end the war. On December 14, 1995, the General Framework Agreement for Peace in Bosnia and Herzegovina (commonly referred to as the Dayton Peace Agreement) was officially signed in Paris, thus bringing an end to the war. More than 250,000 people had been killed in the fighting, while over one million refugees had fled their homes.

Dayton authorized the deployment of the NATO-led Implementation Force (IFOR) and, in December 1995, 60,000 IFOR troops from 29 nations began Operation *Joint Endeavor* to "monitor and enforce compliance with the military aspects of the Peace Agreement."

In 1995, 1-4 Cavalry was the first US unit deployed to Bosnia-Herzegovina, supporting the peacekeeping mission set forth by the Dayton Peace Agreement, using its Black Hawk helicopters to fly troops and equipment around the rugged Bosnian terrain.

Trouble again flared in the former Yugoslavia four years later. Reports of massacres of ethnic Albanian civilians began to trickle out of Kosovo, the southern province of Serbia, early in 1999. The massacres followed brutal counterinsurgency operations undertaken by Yugoslav and Serb forces in Kosovan villages. Belgrade rejected all attempts by the international community to make peace, so on March 24, 1999, NATO launched Operation *Allied Force*, bombing targets from the air in both Yugoslavia and Kosovo.

Yugoslavia eventually agreed to a peace deal. The UN Security Council passed Resolution 1244 on June 10, 1999, putting Kosovo under UN control and the deployment of a 50,000-strong Kosovo Force (KFOR) through Operation *Joint Guardian*.

KFOR originally deployed on June 13, 1999, comprising 50,000 troops from about 35 states, including Russia, although by 2006 this had fallen below 17,000 as KFOR underwent restructuring. Troops are deployed in five multinational task forces (north, west, east, center, and south) and with the KFOR headquarters at Pristina. Each task force includes infantry, reconnaissance, aviation, engineer, and other support elements, with major contributing countries providing mixed detachments rather than specific units.

The main US contribution to KFOR was with the Multinational Task Force (MNTF)(E), centered at the US Army's Camp Bondsteel, outside the former garrison town of Uroševac. The base was the headquarters of Task Force Falcon and Multinational Brigade (East). The US Army's composite aviation battalion had a large helicopter force consisting of ten UH-60A/L Black Hawks, eight AH64A Apaches, eight OH-58D Kiowa Warriors, and a further six UH-60As configured for MEDEVAC duties.

Since the Black Hawks were the only helicopters able to operate in light and moderately icy conditions, they were the most extensively used machines during the harsh Balkan winters. By the end of 2004, the only remaining US forces in the former Yugoslavia were the 1,000 Ohio Army National Guard soldiers of the 37th Armor Brigade.

Afghanistan: Operation *Enduring Freedom*
On Sunday, October 7, 2001, American and British forces began an aerial bombing campaign against Afghanistan, targeting al-Qaeda training camps and their Taliban protectors as a military response to the September 11, 2001, suicide attacks on the United States.

The Northern Alliance, fighting against a Taliban weakened by US bombing and massive defections, captured Mazari Sharif on November 9. It took control of Kabul on November 13, and, by the end of November, a number of the Taliban had fled to Pakistan.

The battle of Tora Bora, involving US, British, and Northern Alliance forces, took place in December 2001 to further destroy the Taliban and suspected al-Qaeda in Afghanistan. Early in March 2002, the US military, along with allied Afghan military forces, conducted a large operation to destroy al-Qaeda in an operation codenamed *Anaconda*. Units involved

Cpl Per Larson, a K-9 handler with the Norwegian Mechanized Battalion, runs with his dog to board the US Army UH-60 Black Hawk Stabilization Force (SFOR) helicopter. SFOR succeeded Implementation Force (IFOR) in 1995, and the first US helicopter units assigned were from the 1st Battalion, 4th Cavalry. (DoD/SrA Sean Worrell)

included the 10th Mountain Division, 101st Airborne Division and US Special Forces, along with British, Canadian, Australian, German, New Zealand, and Afghan troops.

Since January 2006, NATO has taken control of operations in Afghanistan, though the US military also conducts operations separately from NATO as part of Operation *Enduring Freedom* in other parts of Afghanistan.

Helicopters are a key element in operations in Afghanistan, and US helicopter forces provide the majority of rotary-wing capability. Joint Task Force Wings, formed in 2004, incorporates Army and Marine Corps assets into its mission of providing rotary-wing combat support to every corner of Afghanistan.

In 2005, Task Force Wings included the UH-60 Black Hawk helicopters of the 2nd Battalion, 25th Aviation Regiment, 25th Infantry Division (Light); Company B, 193rd Aviation Regiment, Hawaii Army National Guard; and aeromedical Black Hawks of the 68th Medical Evacuation Company (Air Ambulance). They served alongside Army and National Guard CH-47 Chinooks and AH-64 Apaches, US Marine Corps CH-53 Super Stallions, AH-1 Cobras, and UH-1 Hueys.

The helicopters performed the full range of rotary-wing missions, from getting a fire team from its base camp to a landing zone through medical evacuation missions and close-air support to providing the logistical support necessary to keep the coalition moving forward. The Joint Task Force has been involved in just about every major operation that has gone on in Afghanistan. Without the helicopters, US and NATO troops would be limited in their mobility by the Afghan terrain, among the most rugged in the world.

Task Force Saber, based at Bagram and Salerno, and Task Force Storm, flying out of Kandahar Airfield, each have CH-47 Chinooks, UH-60 Black Hawks, and AH-64 Apaches in their arsenals. Chinooks are the big haulers, carrying personnel and supplies to far-flung locations. According to Task Force Saber's executive officer, "The Black Hawk is the SUV of the task force, moving troops into combat or casualties out, flying combat missions into hot landing zones ... it does it all."

Iraq: Operation *Iraqi Freedom*
Army aviation was central to the success of the initial combat phase of Operation *Iraqi Freedom* in March 2003. Helicopters flew countless missions in support of ground units in contact or moving in tactical convoys. They moved personnel, equipment, and supplies through the entire widely dispersed battle area.

A UH-60 Black Hawk helicopter departs on a mission from Bagram Airfield, Afghanistan, on March 22, 2007. Nestled amid the highest mountains on Earth, and with a climate ranging from scorching desert heat to arctic winter, Afghanistan challenges the endurance of aircraft and crews alike. (USA/TSgt Cecilio M. Ricardo Jr.)

After major resistance was eliminated, helicopter units occupied fixed bases and became the primary movers of critical supplies until effective ground transportation could be established.

Army aviation attack and cavalry units conducted reconnaissance and security, movement-to-contact, search and attack, and close-combat attack operations in support of the rapid advance of the 3rd Infantry Division.

Army aviation lift and assault helicopter units conducted air assaults; air movement of personnel, supplies, and equipment; and insertion and extraction missions of soldiers at critical locations on the battlefield. Aviation units also supported the commitment of the V Corps reserve and conducted attacks against the Medina Division of Iraq's Republican Guard.

Assault, lift, and medical evacuation units were invaluable to both the ground forces and other aviation units. These units conducted command-and-control and embedded personnel recovery missions; transported downed aircraft recovery teams; moved mission-essential equipment; conducted general support and medical evacuation flights; inserted and extracted long-range surveillance detachments; established forward arming and refueling points (FARP); and conducted air assault operations and refuel missions known as Fat Cow (CH-47) and Fat Hawk (UH-60) operations.

Possibly the most noteworthy helicopter mission took place as the 3rd Infantry Division thrust north toward Baghdad. The 101st Airborne Division's aviation units were tasked with moving an airborne brigade into position to attack elements of the Republican Guard's Medina Division. This meant that the brigade had to move nearly 250 miles north from its staging base in Kuwait.

As the 3rd Infantry Division began to push north, the 101st was tasked with clearing towns and cities in the north of Iraq. The aviation brigades of both divisions supported battalion combat teams with air assaults into these locations, with the final air assault into Mosul spanning more than 310 miles.

By mid-October 2003, Army helicopters in Operation *Iraqi Freedom* had accumulated over 409,000 flying hours. The mix of crude air defenses and Man-Portable Air Defense Systems encountered in the major combat phase and continuing insurgency had claimed 11 aircraft and 32 lives. The desert environment has also taken a toll on Army helicopters. Blade erosion is common, and maintenance personnel found one Black Hawk carrying 35lb of sand under a radio console.

ABOVE LEFT
A US Army Black Hawk arrives to move a team from 45 Commando, Royal Marines to set up a checkpoint in southern Afghanistan during Operation *Buzzard*. American helicopters are a vital component in operations in the region, with Task Force Wings based at Bagram, near Kabul, providing combat support to NATO and US troops all over Afghanistan. (UK MOD)

ABOVE RIGHT
A US Army door gunner mans an M60 7.62mm machine gun at the open door of a UH-60 Black Hawk at Kirkuk Air Base. Door gunners have proved to be as essential in fighting the insurgent war in Iraq as they ever were in delivering troops into "hot" landing zones in Vietnam. (DoD/SSgt Suzanne M. Day, USAF)

A US Army soldier watches for enemy action as troops from Delta Company, 2nd Battalion, 7th Cavalry Regiment board a US Army UH-60 Black Hawk helicopter following a cordon and search operation in Tall Aswad, Iraq, on January 12, 2007. (US Army/SFC Robert C. Brogan)

Black Hawks have continued to play their part in the years since the fall of Saddam Hussein. Regular Army units have been joined by Army Reserve and National Guard companies. According to an Army Reserve company commander, speaking in 2004, "The majority of our missions are to move personnel and equipment in the Baghdad area of operations by air. By moving passengers and equipment by air, we greatly reduce the improvised explosive devices (IED) threat to our forces, keeping our troops safe and ready to fight."

Early in 2007, it was estimated that Army helicopters averaged 100 enemy firefights monthly and were hit about 17 times a month. Generally, the helicopters can return to base, a testament to the quality of pilots, crews, and equipment. The number of flight hours for the Army has nearly doubled in the past two years. In 2005, pilots logged about 240,000 hours, and, in 2006, pilots and crews flew 334,000 hours.

Army helicopters are increasingly being used to support the rebuilding of the Iraqi Army. In July 2006, carried in two lifts by more than 20 UH-60 Black Hawk helicopters of the US Army, more than 400 men of the 1st Mechanized Brigade, 9th Iraqi Army Division conducted a large air assault operation to capture members of a roadside bomb-making cell north of Baghdad.

However, operations are not without risk. The US Army has lost more than 120 helicopters in the war, about 25 percent of them due to enemy engagements. The majority of the firefights involve machine-gun and cannon fire, but man-portable, surface-to-air missiles have been used as well. To avoid potential missile attacks, helicopter pilots fly low and fast.

The biggest threat to helicopters may come from rocket-propelled grenades. Designed to penetrate tank armor, they can be devastating even to the toughest of helicopters. In October 2004, Iraqi insurgents first used a rocket-propelled grenade to bring down a UH-60 Black Hawk helicopter over Tikrit. Two months later, two US helicopters crashed after being hit by ground fire, killing 17 soldiers on board. At least one of the Black Hawks had been hit by a rocket-propelled grenade. This caused the pilot to lose control, colliding in midair with his wingman, bringing both of them down.

Humanitarian relief

The US Army operates dedicated helicopters worldwide for the medical evacuation of injured soldiers and the assistance of the civilian population in time of crisis. This fleet is manned by Active Army, Army Reserve, and Army

F **MEDEVAC IN IRAQ**

One of the most important missions flown by the Black Hawk is medical evacuation. All UH-60s can be converted to carry litters, but the specialized air ambulance variants have an extensive fit of medical equipment. The handful of UH-60Qs and their successors, the HH-60Ls, are fitted with all-weather radar systems and a forward-looking infrared turret to allow rescue missions to be carried out in all weathers and terrains. Aircraft operating in Iraq and Afghanistan have the additional problem of dealing with the all-pervading dust, kicked up in large clouds every time a helicopter lands or takes off.

The threat from insurgents in Iraq, together with the harsh operating conditions, had seen more than 120 US Army helicopters destroyed in Iraq by 2007. This Black Hawk crashed at the Tallil Air Base in 2006. It is a testament to the UH-60's extraordinary toughness that all four soldiers on board survived the crash. (USAF/A1C Jeff Andrejcik)

National Guard personnel. Active military troops support individual states through Military Assistance to Safety and Traffic (MAST). The National Guard has a federal mission to reinforce the Army and a state mission to provide disaster relief.

The Guard provided comfort to Colombians during a volcano eruption, to Somalis during famine, to Californians through earthquakes, and to Kurdish refugees in their time of need. The 101st Air Assault Division provided 1993 snowstorm relief. The 25th Infantry Division (Light) used their utility aircraft to combat the ravages of Hurricane Iniki in Hawaii, and the Black Hawks of the 82nd Airborne Division teamed with the Florida Army National Guard Black Hawks to provide Hurricane Andrew relief.

Most recently, Black Hawks of the National Guard and the 82nd Airborne Division provided relief to New Orleans and the Gulf Coast after Hurricane Katrina in August 2005.

BLACK HAWK OPERATORS

The Black Hawk has been widely exported since it became operational with the US Army in 1978. The S-70A helicopter is the export version of the multimission Black Hawk, and variants of the helicopter are operational or have been ordered by 22 international customers.

Although the Black Hawk is a highly capable successor to the Huey, it has drawbacks that have made it less successful commercially than it might have been. It is more expensive to acquire and to operate than the Huey and is a more complicated machine. For most civilian utility roles and for some foreign militaries, the S-70 is larger and more sophisticated than needed.

The biggest foreign user is South Korea, with 100 UH-60Ps in service. These are basically similar to the UH-60L. The first was delivered from Sikorsky late in 1990, with the next 19 assembled by Korean Air from kits provided by Sikorsky, and the rest have been built in Korea.

Japan

Mitsubishi has license-built a search-and-rescue version of the UH-60L designated the UH-60J. It was acquired to replace the Kawasaki-Vertol KV-107 Sea Knight in Japanese service. The UH-60J variant features external fuel tanks on upswept ESSS mounts, an external rescue winch, Japanese-built radar, a FLIR turret in the nose, and bubble side windows for observers.

Sikorsky delivered two S-70A-12 aircraft as patterns, followed by two more in kit form that were assembled by Mitsubishi. From then onward, construction was by Mitsubishi, with the T700 engines license-built in Japan by Ishikawajima-Harima. The first Mitsubishi-built machine was delivered in early 1991, and the Black Hawk became operational in 1992.

In 1995, the Japanese Ground Self-Defense Force (JGSDF) ordered a utility variant of the UH-60L from Mitsubishi. Given the designation UH-60JA, the airframe is basically that of the UH-60L. However, Japanese military Black Hawks have improved avionics, including FLIR, color weather radar, GPS navigation receiver, and a NVG-compatible cockpit. The first evaluation machine was delivered in 1997. The JGSDF plans to obtain 70 UH-60JAs.

Australia

Australia obtained a single S-70A-9 Black Hawk from Sikorsky, which served as a pattern for license production of 38 examples of the type by Hawker de Havilland. These machines were originally assigned to the Royal Australian Air Force but later transferred to the Australian Army. They are basically UH-60Ls with HIRSS exhausts, cable cutters, the SH-60 Seahawk automatic flight control system and folding stabilator, an external rescue hoist, and some Australian-manufactured electronics.

In the 1990s, Sikorsky offered a heavily armed version of the Black Hawk in the Australian Army's Air 87 armed reconnaissance helicopter program. Known as the AH-60L or the S-70 Battle Hawk, its major weapons feature was the 20mm GIAT THL 20 turreted 20mm cannon, located under the cabin. It could be sighted by an Elbit Systems Helmet Mounted Display (HMD) or by a Toplite targeting sensor. Other weapons offered included Hellfire missiles, 2.75-in. rockets, Stinger missiles, and various gun pods including 7.65mm, 20mm, and 30mm cannon.

Unfortunately for Sikorsky, the Battle Hawk did not make the Australian short list. The Eurocopter Tiger, an armed reconnaissance helicopter in the 6,000kg class, was selected under the Air 87 program for service with the Australian Army.

A UH-60P Black Hawk helicopter of the Republic of Korea Forces comes in for a landing at Tak San Ri Beach near Pohang, South Korea, in support of Exercise *Foal Eagle* in 2000. (DoD/TSgt James E. Lotz, USAF)

Israel

Israel received ten US Army surplus Black Hawks in July 1994, free of charge. The Israeli Air Force later purchased 24 new-build UH-60Ls, which were delivered in 2002.

Saudi Arabia

Saudi Arabia has obtained 21 Desert Hawks, including 12 S-70A-1 machines configured as utility transports, one S-70A-1 configured as a VIP transport, and eight S-70A-1L MEDEVAC machines. The utility transports can be fitted with French GIAT 20mm cannon on pintle mounts, while the MEDEVAC machines have an external hoist, provision for six litters, and a searchlight.

Turkey

Turkey obtained 12 S-70A-17s for police and paramilitary police forces, including two VIP machines, followed by a larger order in the 1990s for S-70A-28 machines. Ultimately, Turkey hopes to operate up to 200 Black Hawks.

An Australian Army Black Hawk from the 5th Aviation Regiment is prepared for an underslung load as part of a humanitarian mission in Pakistan following the devastating earthquake that struck the region in October 2005. (Australian Department of Defence)

Most or all of the S-70A-28 machines were delivered with or upgraded to a digital glass cockpit. Apparently one was hit by a rocket-propelled grenade during an action against Kurdish insurgents in the east of Turkey: the helicopter continued to fly and made it back to base with a gaping hole in the tail boom.

Miscellaneous

Other nations have obtained the Black Hawk in small quantities. Britain is not a formal user of the Black Hawk, but one S-70A-16 was supplied to Rolls-Royce for testing Rolls/Turbomeca TRM-332 turboshaft engines, and a single S-70A-19 was supplied to Westland preparatory to a license production deal that fell through. The Westland-built Black Hawks were to be assigned the WS-70 designation.

Black Hawks have been sold to a number of Middle Eastern countries in addition to Israel and Saudi Arabia. Bahrain has a single S-70A-14 Black Hawk, similar to the UH-60L but fitted out as a luxury VIP transport. Egypt bought two S-70A-21 Black Hawks, and Jordan acquired three S-70A-11 helicopters.

Far Eastern operators include Hong Kong, which has two S-70A-27 Black Hawks. The Philippines obtained two S-70A-5 models. Thailand has two S-70A-6 utility machines and two S-70A-20 VIP transports.

Morocco obtained two S-70A-26 Black Hawks, while Mexico flies two similar S-70A-24s.

Sikorsky sold an S-70C version of the Black Hawk that was supposedly for civilian use, but most are flown in a military or paramilitary role. Brunei obtained one S-70C as a VIP transport. The People's Republic of China operates 24 S-70C-2 utility machines. They are among the most capable rotorcraft in China's inventory. More powerful than Chinese-built variants of

 1. AUSTRALIAN AH-60

Australian Black Hawks were originally operated by the Royal Australian Air Force as shown here, but a rationalization of the nation's defenses has seen the type transferred to Army control. Black Hawks have been used extensively in Iraq and Afghanistan and for humanitarian relief missions in areas as diverse as the Pakistani Himalayas and the coasts of Indonesia and Thailand. An armed version of the Black Hawk known as the Battle Hawk was offered to the Australians in the 1990s, but the Department of Defence chose to buy the Eurocopter Tiger. Similarly, when the Australian Army decided to update its helicopter force, it preferred the European MRH 90 over the UH-60M offered by Sikorsky.

2. ISRAELI UH-60

Israel acquired its first ten UH-60s as a gift from the United States in 1994, and later bought 24 more aircraft. Known as Yanshuf (Hebrew for "owl"), the type is operated by the 124th "Rolling Sword" Squadron at Palmachim, as seen here, and by the 123rd Squadron at Hatzerim. Unlike other Israeli helicopters, which are generally painted in desert colors, most Israeli Black Hawks retain the US Helicopter Green paint scheme. This often looks much darker in photographs, possibly due to the bright sun and dry climate in which the images are taken. In the year 2000, several helicopters were tested with a brown/sand desert camouflage scheme, but though generally successful it was not adopted.

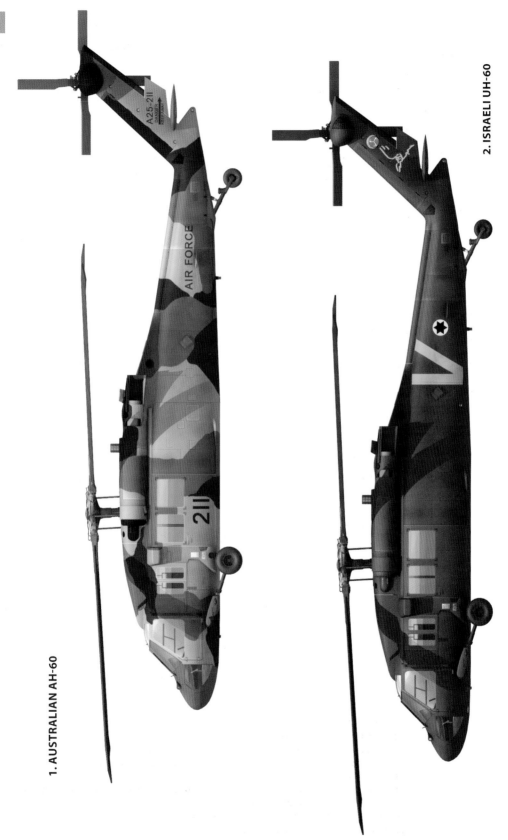

1. AUSTRALIAN AH-60

2. ISRAELI UH-60

US Marines serving with landing force Cooperation Afloat Readiness and Training (CARAT) offload a Royal Brunei Air Force UH-60 Black Hawk helicopter as part of a food resupply mission during an exercise in 2002. Brunei operates one Black Hawk as a VIP transport, together with two further utility machines. (DoD/LCpl Antonio J. Vega, USMC)

old Soviet designs, they have been used in the high-altitude regions of Tibet where their greater performance was a distinct advantage. Taiwan also received S-70Cs, 14 equipped with external rescue hoists being acquired for search-and-rescue duties.

Recent orders include two further Black Hawks for the Royal Brunei Force, two S-70As configured for executive transport for Malaysia, a further 50 S-70As for Turkey, nine for Austria, 30 for Colombia, 24 for Israel, and two for Thailand. In July 2004, the Royal Jordanian Air Force ordered eight helicopters to enter service in 2006. In September 2004, Brazil requested a Foreign Military Sale of ten UH-60L helicopters.

In July 2005, Colombia requested eight more helicopters and the Royal Thai Navy two. In June 2006, the United Arab Emirates requested 26 helicopters under the Foreign Military Sales program, and Bahrain expressed an interest in nine UH-60Ms. In July 2006, Saudi Arabia requested 24 UH-60Ls, and, in September, Colombia requested a further 15 UH-60Ls.

Saudi Arabia was one of the first customers for the export variant of the Black Hawk, the S-70A. Most serve with the 1st Aviation Battalion at King Khalid Military City, but eight medically configured S-70A1Ls are operated by the Saudi Armed Forces Medical Services at the same base. (Cody Images)

An S-70A-39 Black Hawk of the Fuerza Aérea de Chile comes in to land. The Chilean Air Force acquired a single export version of the Black Hawk in 1998. It is operated by the Grupo de Aviación No. 9 from the Los Cerrillos Air Base at Santiago. (Cody Images)

APPENDIX

The following list annotates the numerous variants of the Sikorsky Black Hawk UH-60.

S-70
Sikorsky company designation for the UH-60.

UH-60A Black Hawk
Original US Army version, carrying a crew of three to four, and up to 11 passengers. Equipped with T-700-GE-700 engines.

UH-60A "Pot Hawk"
Antidrug surveillance model for the US Customs Service.

UH-60A Credible Hawk
Early search-and-rescue model for the US Air Force.

GUH-60A
Ground instructional model not equipped for flight.

JUH-60A
Test aircraft.

UH-60A RASCAL
NASA-modified version for the Rotorcraft-Aircrew Systems Concepts Airborne Laboratory program for the study of helicopter maneuverability.

EH-60A Black Hawk
Stations for two electronic systems mission operators.

MH-60A Black Hawk
Known as Velcro Hawk; modified with additional avionics, precision navigation system, FLIR, and air-to-air refueling capability.

UH-60B
Proposed model with new engines and an upgraded cockpit. Not built.

YEH-60B Black Hawk
UH-60A prototype for stand-off target acquisition system.

YSH-60B Seahawk
Developmental version of SH-60B.

SH-60B Seahawk
"Navalized" version for US Navy.

NSH-60B Seahawk
Flight test airframe.

UH-60C Black Hawk
Modified version for command-and-control missions.

EH-60C Black Hawk
Redesignation of EH-60A.

HH-60D Nighthawk
Advanced combat search-and-rescue model for the US Air Force. Canceled.

CH-60E
Proposed assault transport helicopter for the US Marine Corps. Not built.

VH-60D Nighthawk
VIP-configured UH-60A, used for presidential transport. T-700-GE-401 engines. Later redesignated VH-60N.

HH-60E
Proposed simpler and less expensive version of the HH-60D. Not built.

SH-60F Seahawk
Upgraded Navy variant equipped with dipping sonar.

NSH-60F Seahawk
Modified SH-60F to support the VH-60N Cockpit Upgrade Program.

HH-60G Pave Hawk
Modified UH-60A primarily designed for combat search and rescue. Equipped with rescue hoist and retractable in-flight refueling probe.

MH-60G Pave Hawk
Special operations version, equipped with long-range fuel tanks, air-to-air refueling capability, FLIR, improved radar. T-700-GE-700/701 engines.

HH-60H Seahawk
Modified SH-60F with both offensive and defensive weaponry. T-700-GE-401 engines.

HH-60J Jayhawk
US Coast Guard version, equipped with rescue hoist.
UH-60J
Japanese utility helicopter similar to the UH-60L but optimized for search and rescue.
MH-60K Black Hawk
Modified special operations variant used by the 160th Special Operations Aviation Regiment.
UH-60L Black Hawk
UH-60A with upgraded T-700-GE-701C engines, improved gearbox, and additional vibration absorbers.
EUH-60L
Modified with additional mission electronic equipment for Army Airborne Command and Control.
EH-60L Black Hawk
Upgraded EH-60A.
HH-60L
UH-60L extensively modified with medical mission equipment. Rescue hoist.
MH-60L Direct Action Penetrator (DAP)
Special operations modification, operated by the 160th Special Operations Aviation Regiment. Can be armed with a variety of weapons including 30mm chain gun and 2.75-in. rockets.
AH-60L Arpía III
Export version for Colombia, used by the Fuerza Aérea Colombiana.
AH-60L Battle Hawk
Export version proposed for the Australian Army.

UH-60M Black Hawk
UH-60L upgraded with improved design wide chord rotor system, T-700-GE-701D engines, improved durability gearbox, and modern glass cockpit.
HH-60M
UH-60M with medical mission equipment.
VH-60N Presidential Hawk
US Marine Corps VIP model equipped with extensive avionics and communications equipment.
UH-60P Black Hawk
Export version for the Republic of Korea, similar to UH-60L.
UH-60Q Black Hawk
UH-60A modified for medical evacuation.
YMH-60R Seahawk
Prototype for MH-60R. T-700-GE-701C engines.
MH-60R Seahawk
Modified multimission SH-60B. T-700-GE-401 engines.
SH-60R Seahawk
Modified SH-60B with improved radar and sonar.
NSH-60R Seahawk
US Navy test platform. T-700-GE-701C engines.
CH-60S Seahawk
Proposed upgrade of UH-60L and SH-60R for cargo transport.
MH-60S
Navy medical evacuation and ship replenishment variant. T-700-GE-401 engines.

OPPOSITE The Sikorsky UH-60 Black Hawk has been the mainstay of the US Army's tactical transport fleet for more than a quarter of a century. It has seen combat wherever America has gone to war and will remain a frontline warrior well into the 21st century. (Sikorsky)

LEFT US Navy sailors aboard the Wasp-class amphibious assault ship USS *Bataan* (LHD 5) stand by with chocks and chains as two US Army UH-60M Black Hawk helicopters of the 160th Special Operations Aviation Regiment prepare to land on board the flight deck. The Special Forces variants of the latest Black Hawk are seen in February 2006, while undergoing their over water qualification program. (DoD/Photographer's Mate Pedro A. Rodriguez, USN)

INDEX

References to illustration captions are shown in **bold**.